Zelda's
Moments
with
Mom

Other Books by Carol Gardner and Shane Young

Zelda Wisdom

The Zen of Zelda

Zelda Rules on Love

Zelda's Survival Guide

Zelda's Tips from the Tub

Zelda's Bloopers

Also by Carol Gardner

Bumper Sticker Wisdom

Zelda's Moments with Mom

Memories a Mother Never Forgets

Carol Gardner and Shane Young

A Zelda Wisdom™ Book

**Andrews McMeel
Publishing**

Kansas City

07 08 09 10 TWP 10 9 8 7 6 5 4 3 2

ISBN-13: 978-0–7407–5710-5
ISBN-10: 0-7407-5710-5

Library of Congress Control Number: 2005932619

www.andrewsmcmeel.com

Attention: Schools and Businesses
Andrews McMeel books are available at quantity discounts with bulk purchase for educational, business, or sales promotional use. For information, please write to: Special Sales Department, Andrews McMeel Publishing, LLC, 4520 Main Street, Kansas City, Missouri 64111.

This book is dedicated to my mother,
Ardyce Wik Lentz.

Growing up, you don't really think much about your mother. After all, she is always there for you ... with love, with happiness, with healing, and with humor. I hesitate to make the parallel, but our mothers are a lot like our dogs ... the unconditional love givers. Maybe that's why we need them so much. Maybe that's why we love them so much. Sometimes we forget to thank our mothers and tell them how important and wonderful they are, or were. We know they are there for us to come home to, to share dreams with, and to cry with when those dreams happen and when they don't.

About ten years ago my wonderful mother was in a car accident that has left her in a semi-coma. How many times have I sat by her bedside and wished I could tell her how much her love meant? We are what our mothers make us. My mother taught me how to survive tough times, to savor the good times, and to value friends and family. Her love and faith gave me the self-confidence to always try, no matter how difficult the task. She taught me to love with an open hand.

This book comes as a thank-you to my mother for her sacrifices, for the fun she shared, and for the lessons and wisdom she taught. I can't return all of that, but I can try to share those memories in Zelda's Moments with Mom.

Here's to the best mother ever. This one's for you. Thanks with all my heart.

Carol

*Carol's mother, Ardyce Wik Lentz, died on October 2, 2005, in Carol's arms. Her mother had seen the mock-up of Zelda's Moments with Mom prior to her passing.

Let your children go
if you want to keep them.

—Malcolm Forbes

Memories a Mother Never Forgets

Think back to your childhood. Who was always there for you? Mom! Sometimes it's hard to find just the right words to tell her how you feel and how much you appreciate all that unconditional love. In Zelda's Moments with Mom we've tried to express those thoughts by re-creating many of the memories.

In "Early Moments" we start from the beginning ... with babies. Most women want babies, but are they prepared for the reality of it all? Stinky diapers, no sleep, nonstop nursing and crying. Talk about a tough job. Yet, there is no better job, nor is there a job more rewarding.

To put this book together we used several absolutely adorable little bulldog puppies who impersonated babies. The puppies ranged from Angus to ZeeZee. In between there was Dan, Diesel, Russell, and Wally, not to mention their mom and my friend, Daphne. You might say Daphne was the role model for this book. In the beginning I was just an observer not wanting to get in the way of nipples. As the puppies progressed in age I stepped in and what fun we had. Try putting three puppies in a shopping cart! What about four puppies wearing shower caps in a bathtub? We ended up with only one in the tub and considered ourselves lucky. It was a lot like any early childhood. Chaos was common!

The art of being a mother so impressed us that we went back in history to look at some "Memorable Mothers," starting with Mother Earth and ending with Mother Teresa. After all, motherhood and sainthood should be synonymous. I must admit that impersonating the Queen Mother was my favorite role. Now there was a mother who ruled!

Our last chapter is made up of "Moments to Remember." Here's where I get a little teary-eyed, because this chapter is about times in a mother's life that are indelible. Some memories, like saying good-bye on the first day of school or reading a bedtime story and not wanting it to end, will always stay with a mother.

Motherhood is loving with an intensity that life doesn't prepare you for. Of course raising children isn't always easy. But the good news is that Mother Nature is providential. She gives mothers twelve years before turning her little darlings into devilish teenagers. The truly amazing thing about motherhood is that even middle-aged children have mothers who are still looking for ways to improve them. To our mothers, we are always children. As children we may leave home, but we always take our mothers' hearts with us.

So this book is for our mothers. They molded our minds and, with luck, turned us into adults. We love you!

Zelda

CHAPTER

1

Early
Moments

No one prepares you for the miracle of childbirth. Whether it's a girl or a boy, the beauty of your own baby is beyond words, even when the face is one only a mother could love.

While being a mother is the most important job you'll ever hold, being a "new" mother is also the hardest job you'll ever encounter.

From the beginning you think you are in control. Yet, it's "Have buggy, let's boogey...baby in charge!"

"Mother load" takes on a new meaning. There are times when motherhood seems nothing more than feeding the mouth that bites you. Recognize that look of total exhaustion?

What once seemed simple is now difficult. Did you truly want to add all three to your shopping cart?

Every night it seems as if they are awake and waiting for Santa, while you are just waiting for a little sleep. Ah, the magic of motherhood.

But then there are the moments when you plant your dreams and watch with pride as your little bit of happiness grows.

Mothers are here to tell their children they're beautiful, and if they aren't, it doesn't matter. The sweetest flower doesn't have to be the prettiest.

What mother hasn't chanted, "Rub-a-dub-dub, if I can only get you in the tub? And by the way, don't even think of drinking the bathwater!"

For every mother her daughter
is her little princess, or...

her son is her little prince,
whether or not they are a royal pain
or a royal pride.

Some days they are just little stinkers.

Most of the time, however,
they are your "sweet pea" or . . .

your little "punkin."

Being a mother means taking time to teach that it's not how much you have to enjoy, it's how much you enjoy what you have . . . like time together.

Being a mother also means
enthusiastically sharing dreams,
however unrealistic, as in, "When I
grow up I'm going to be a cowboy."

When a sibling arrives
a mother has the tough job
of being the impartial referee
in "double-dog-dare-ya" disputes.

Sometimes she has to remind herself
that boys will be boys, and . . .

being the "bruise brothers"
is part of growing up.

In those early moments,
children learn that "Mother May I?"
is much more than a game.
It's a reality.

Memorable Mothers

In the beginning there was Mother Earth. She taught us the value of Birkenstocks and granola, and that "litter" was bad and shouldn't be confused with a group of newborn puppies.

Then along came Mother Nature, who was providential and gave us twelve years to develop enough love for our children before turning them into teenagers.

We all know that necessity
was the Mother of Invention.
The father is still unknown.

Mother Goose was our first introduction to poetry. She taught us that a cow can jump over the moon and maybe we can even jump over candlesticks. Jumping through hoops we had to learn on our own.

Then there's Whistler's Mother. If you asked Whistler he'd probably say, "If it wasn't one thing, it was my mother." Isn't it true that in therapy the correct answer is always, "Because of my mother"?

One thing all mothers know
is that every mother
is a Queen Mother.

Many believe Mother Teresa to be a saint. After all, motherhood and sainthood should be synonymous.

CHAPTER

3

Moments with Mom

Mom, you were the one who read me
those bedtime stories...
and I was the one who pleaded,
"Just one more, pleeeze."

Every morning you woke up
to a new challenge ... me!
But many mornings you woke up
to my morning kisses.

You were also there
when I didn't want to get up.

You healed my wounds, both physical and psychological. And you taught me that sometimes laughter is the best medicine.

You were there for me when
tough sledding was ahead.
And you taught me that
success is not an accident,
but takes hanging on.

It made me happy when people said
I looked like you.

Thanks for sharing and pulling my wagon, no matter how heavy the load. And . . .

thanks for showing me, by example, how to turn lemons into lemonade.

I'll never forget how you hid your tears
on my first day of school and
pretended not to notice mine.

You helped me put on my raincoat and taught me about weathering storms. You told me that storms never last and that there would always be sunshine if we just waited.

Whenever I was feeling blue,
your chocolate chip cookies
appeared out of nowhere.
You thought of me while I was
busy thinking of myself.

Do you remember calling me
your armchair quarterback?
You supplied the popcorn and put up
with me being a little remote.

Not only were you a great soccer mom, but you taught me that I'd always miss 100 percent of the goals I didn't try to kick. I'm still "kicking" whenever I see opportunities.

Can I confess to you now?
When we went camping I was afraid
of the dark and of those scary noises
outside the tent. But as long as
you were there, I felt safe.

You taught me that if I didn't make mistakes I wouldn't make anything and that I really wouldn't make anything if I didn't finish my homework.

Then there was my "I'm going to be different" stage. Thanks for not reminding me of it or sharing the photos. Can we just laugh about it now?

As you may recall I'm sure
my skateboarding gave you
some sleepless nights,
as did my learning to drive.

You were my cheerleader,
and I could count on you
to root for me
even when I was losing.

Thanks for teaching me
to play fair and that I didn't have
to be ruthless to be competitive.

I knew you were never more
than a phone call away.

Mirror, mirror on the wall . . .
I am my mother after all.

Plato and Socrates
were just quoting their mothers.

Thanks Mom.